365

Days of Gratitude

My Attitude of Gratitude

Muskan Virk

Dear Sindy

With Love
Muskan Virk

HELPING HANDS PUBLISHING

First Published in Vancouver, BC, Canada in 2016 by
Helping Hands Publishing

ISBN: 978-0-692-76556-2

First Edition

Foreword

Growing up with parents who were spiritual and who had lived their lives in the most courageous way was how I saw life unfold before me. One of the things that they have always instilled in us is that we are the creators of our destiny. Part of that is consciousness in gratitude. Being grateful for each and every single experience that we may have encountered in our journey. Each of these inspires a lesson, brings a message, and in turn, is crafted and molded into life experience.

The word gratitude, with its Latin roots "gratus," is thankfulness. What does it mean to be thankful? To be grateful for each experience that's in our destiny? The words in this book say and inspire just that. Muskan captured the true essence of gratefulness she had created in her life. With the inspiration of this book stemming from something that she was so compelled to pursue, to address and to use that energy to make a difference is truly inspiring. As you flip through the pages and realize that each grateful thought and each set of words transforms into the pure meaning of simply being thankful each day, that practice is something we should all aspire to achieve in our lives.

My father, Wayne, had said, "Be in a state of gratitude for everything that shows up in your life. Be thankful for the storms, as well as the smooth sailing. What is the lesson or gift in what you are experiencing right now? Find your joy not in what's missing in your life, but in how you can serve." How can we continually be of service not just for others, but also, most importantly, for ourselves? As we challenge ourselves into living a full life and lifting ourselves into higher consciousness, we must propel into a life of service and being in a state of gratitude. This is a practice where you will be challenged in some way. However, with challenges comes growth and learning on how to be a better version of our self. In turn, that knowledge is something we can share with others as well. In this book, the subtitle "My Attitude of Gratitude" really speaks to the mindset and intention Muskan had set forth when writing her thoughts.

It's true that our attitude guides our thoughts and then the actions we choose. Her thoughts show how finding gratefulness in simplicity has a far greater impact without complexity. Whether it's a freshly-baked cookie or the sound of birds in the backyard, she had found the true beauty in these and was able to extract the exact reason on why these resonated with her. Gratefulness brings the appreciation of experiences that we may think are everyday routine, yet this is truly the sole purpose of practicing gratefulness in each day. As we live our present journey, being grateful brings a whole perspective into the experience of life, light, and love. The joy of blessings that we are meant to experience and that we invite into our lives is something in itself to be grateful for. I invite you to experience these thoughts of gratitude that Muskan has so lovingly shared with the universe. Surrender to the sweet joy of gratefulness in each and every day.

~ Serena Dyer ~

Photo by: Cengiz Ozelzel, Adagion Studio

In memory of Alexa Middelaer – may your memory inspire each of us to be grateful for every day.
To support Alexa's legacy, we invite you to learn about MADD Canada – www.madd.ca

Photo by: Craig Minielly/Aura Photographics

This book is dedicated to all of my grandparents and the history that they gave my Mom and Dad. Thank you for always being there for me. I'm so grateful for your hugs, your stories about how my parents wanted to help people too when they were my age, for being a part of my life and always believing in me. I'm so thankful for all the stories but most of all, I'm thankful for being your grandchild.

Day 1

I am thankful that my family believes in gender equality and I am welcomed and loved as a girl.

Day 2

I am thankful to have such a wonderful Mom who teaches me so much. I feel all the Moms in the world are very special.

My Mom is always loving, and tells me so many stories about all the people who have made a difference in the world.

Day 3

I am thankful for clouds and fog on our beautiful mountains.

Every morning when I go to school, I look at this scene of beautiful mountains, but I love to see all the clouds and fog floating around. It is so wonderful to see this magical scene.

Day 4

I am so thankful for all the bumps and bruises because they teach me a lesson.

Every time I get hurt, I get a bump or bruise; it teaches me to be careful next time. They are my teachers.

Day 5

I am so thankful to have a great Nana.

She gives me so much love and hugs. She makes my favorite food. She is a good mind reader because she always knows to cook the food that I love.

Day 6

I am so thankful to be a CHILD.

I have so much fun being a kid. I can eat candies and just do fun things.

Day 7

I am very thankful to have a Dad who always loves me.

I know some people don't have a Dad. So, that makes me think how important it is to have a Dad who loves me.

Day 8

I am thankful for my gratitude.

Today, what are you grateful for? I invite you to fill this page with everything you are grateful for.

Day 9

I am thankful for the silence in chess games. I love playing chess. Silence helps me to plan what move I should make next.

I am most grateful to be a Mom. It is the best thing that has ever happened to me. Being a Mom has taught me to be more patient, present, and compassionate and has helped me to be a better leader in my work. It has also taught me the importance of self-care, so I can be there for my daughter to help her when she needs me most. Being a Mom has also connected me to my inner child and brought back play and fun to balance out my hard working personality type and make me laugh when life leaves an irritating rock in my shoe. Most of all, being a Mom has brought me to a greater purpose, an appreciation for all life, and an everlasting bond with my child, which brings me such contentment and happiness.

Photo by: Jennifer Strang Photography

~ Maya Kanigan, Women In Leadership ~

For the past 15 years, Maya Kanigan has been creating and directing solutions to advance women in leadership and empower the next generation through a national, non-profit organization with charity status that she founded and successfully implemented in 2001. Maya founded the Women in Leadership Foundation (WIL) to create awareness of the shortage of women in leadership roles, to produce a platform for conversation on leadership topics and to help women overcome barriers to succeed

From 2004 to 2010, her work with WIL was centred around delivering labour market projects through studies on the attraction, recruitment and retention of women with partnerships with the federal and provincial governments, and industry and corporate sectors.
Maya's newest project is LeadingTalent.ca – Canada's first career resource and job portal for top female talent, which will officially launch in March 2016.

Maya holds a Bachelor of Commerce degree from the University of Victoria and, in 2015, was awarded the Gustavson School of Business *25 Alumni to Watch* honour. In 2007, she won a scholarship to participate in the Rotman School of Management's Judy Project – a development program for high potential leaders.

Born on March 8th - International Women's Day - Maya is a high performance leader with a passion to make a difference. She is a proud Mom of daughter Bella and is teaching her Russian.

Day 10

I am so thankful to just play around in my house.

I know there are so many kids around the world who never had a chance to play because they have to work.

Day 11

I am thankful to all living creatures on this earth. There are so many beautiful animals and birds on this planet. It amazes me to see how they are different and beautiful at the same time.

Day 12

I am thankful to rise early every morning.

We get up early, and I love it because by the time I reach school, I am all ready for school, and also I study at home in the morning before I go to school.

Day 13

I am thankful to all the bunnies who come in our yard.

They're so cute, and I love watching them sitting, eating leaves and hopping around.

Day 14

I am very thankful to have three meals a day. There are so many children who don't have enough food to eat. I always wonder how they must feel, and I really want to help them.

Day 15

I am so thankful for ice cream cakes.

Oh, I love ice cream and ice cream cakes.

They are my favourite treat!

Day 16

I am thankful for the sun coming up after a fog.

What have you seen in nature that you are grateful for? Draw or write about it on this page and share with a friend!

Day 17

I am so thankful for a new day.

It gives me a chance to fix my mistakes of yesterday, and try to do my best living a new day.

Day 18

I am so thankful for the love, hugs and smiles I get every day.

I feel very good after, I feel loved.

Day 19

I am thankful to have paper and pen to write on every day.

I know there are so many kids in the world who don't have a pen and paper.

Day 20

I am very thankful to sleep in a cozy bed every day.

I see so many homeless kids and adults who are not as fortunate as I am. My dream is to help all the homeless people around the world.

Day 21

I am very thankful for the care provided to me when I got sick. Everyone in the hospital was so nice and took very good care of me. Not everyone in this world is lucky to have this kind of care.

Day 22

I am very thankful to have such good family friends.

Our family friends are so nice, it makes me feel blessed.

Day 23

I am thankful for all the warm and cozy clothes. I love to play in the snow, so it's nice to have warm clothes on a snowy day.

Day 24

I am thankful for all the seasons we get. I wonder how it would feel to have just one season.

Day 25

I'm very thankful to travel in good vehicles.

It is a blessing to be able to ride in good vehicles because not everyone has them. In Malala's book, *I Am Malala*, she describes what kind of vehicles they have in her country.

Day 26

I am so thankful to have great roads in my country.

I know it must be hard to travel on broken and uneven roads like the ones that I hear about in stories.

Day 27

I am thankful for chocolate covered blueberries.

They taste so good!

What is your favourite treat? Write it down below, and the next time you have one, share with a friend!

Day 28

I am so thankful to be able to lick a cake bowl!

Whenever my Mom bakes, I love to lick the bowl. It is super fun!

I am

thankful

for

my

healty

body.

Day 29

I am thankful for weekends.

I love going to school, but you need to have some fun, too. No school on weekends, love it!

Day 30

I am thankful for holidays.

We get to travel to places and different parts of the world. I love seeing other countries and learning about them!

What are you thankful for today? Write it down and share it with someone special in your life!

Day 31

I am so thankful for the popcorn and snacks that I get in the movies.

I love food, going to movies and hearing the popcorn pop! Having snacks is fun.

Day 32

I am thankful to have toys to play with.

I know not every kid in the world gets to play with toys.

Day 33

I am thankful for all the presents I get on my birthday.

Opening presents is a lot of fun!

Day 34

I am very thankful for all the play dates.

It gives me a chance to play with my friends and have fun.

Day 35

I am so thankful for my long hair.

I love my long hair! I feel like Princess Jasmine!

Day 36

I am thankful for my Dad! He always takes me to fun places, like the Pacific National Exhibition fair.

It's so much fun!

Day 37

I am so thankful to get Tae Kwon Do lessons.

I want to earn a black belt. That means that I worked hard to get this far.

Day 38

I am thankful to hear that I'm cute.

It is a good feeling to get a compliment.

Day 39

I am thankful to go out and buy some books to read.

Books have so much knowledge, and I love to fill my brain with this knowledge.

Day 40

I am very thankful to all the beautiful flowers in my garden.

I love flowers and sometimes I wonder how they get lovely colours.

Day 41

I am thankful to have a TV.

I think of the kids in the poor countries who do not have TVs, and it makes me feel blessed. I love to watch dancers on TV.

Day 42

I am thankful to see trees full of snow in winter time.

It is just a beautiful sight to see.

Day 43

I am thankful for sunny days.

Well, it rains a lot in Vancouver, so it is so nice to see Mr. Sun once in a while.

Day 44

I am thankful to ride a horse.

I love horses, and it is fun to ride a horse. I talk to them. I think they understand.

Day 45

I am so thankful to see a Canadian flag flying.

I am a proud Canadian! It's so nice to watch our flag in the air.

Day 46

I am so thankful for group hugs.

In my family, we do group hugs, and I love it. We include our dog in it, too.

Day 47

I am thankful to see birds looking for food in the winter.

It is so much fun to see different birds.

What's your favourite bird?

Draw it below!

Day 48

I am thankful to see rainbows in the sky.

They are so fascinating to watch! There are so many different colors in the rainbow, and how and where do they come from?

Day 49

I am thankful for the swimming pools in hotels.

I love to swim. So, every time we stay in a hotel with a pool I get to swim as long as I want.

Day 50

I am so thankful to the people who can give instructions nicely.

It is just so much nicer to deal with people who are polite and nice

Day 51

I am thankful for passing a test.

It makes me feel proud of myself to reach a goal!

Day 52

I am thankful for all the notes that I get from my Mom in my lunch kit. It is hard to describe the feeling.

It feels like my Mom is there telling me, "Keep going. You are doing a good job!" It cheers me up if I am having a rough day in school.

Day 53

I am so thankful to say "sorry" when I hurt someone. Well, it makes me understand that it is not a good thing to get hurt, and I feel proud when I say sorry because it takes a lot of courage to say it.

Day 54

I am so thankful to live each day.

Some kids die early due to an illness or an accident, and sometimes because of an adult who cannot control their anger or they just simply make a very poor choice by killing a child or in fact anyone.

Day 55

I am so thankful for all the lessons that I learn from my parents and teachers. They will help me to be a better person.

Day 56

I am thankful for the variety of foods I get to eat. Some people do not have anything to eat.

What do you like to eat most and why? Write it down below!

Day 57

I am thankful to taste lemon water that my Mom makes.

It tastes good and I appreciate it.

Day 58

I am thankful for the paper planes that my Dad makes.

It is so much fun to play with my Dad.

Day 59

I love to float on my back in the pool and ocean.

I love to swim, and floating is fun.

Write down what you're grateful for today!

Day 60

Have you ever thought about the simple things?

How about having clean water to drink? I am thankful for the clean water that I get to drink.

I have seen on tv and
also heard from my parents that
there are so many people
on this planet who dont
have clean water to drink.
I have seen in some
Photos that people have
travle far to get
water and somtimes
some peopls have
to drink from
puddles. so
that makes me
very appreecative
for what I
have.

Day 61

I am thankful to have Black Forest ham sandwich for lunch today.

This is one of my favorite sandwiches.

Day 62

I am so thankful to have an

immaculate lawn.

It is so nice to sit and play

in a clean yard.

Day 63

I am thankful to have a great day at school today.

I learned a lot and played a lot, too.

Why are you thankful for today?

Note it below, and look back on it when you're having a rough day!

Day 64

I am so thankful to have dinners outside. It is so nice to sit and eat in a restaurant.

Day 65

I am thankful to my parents.

I love my Mom and Dad so much and am very thankful to have them.

Day 66

I am thankful for cell phones.

It is a great way to stay connected with your family.

Day 67

I am so thankful for all the food samples at the grocery store. It is fun to try new things.

Day 68

I am very thankful to accept a compliment.

It is polite to say, “Thank you” when someone gives a compliment. I love to give compliments and receive them too.

Day 69

I am so thankful to have clean clothes every day. Well, it is a good feeling to wear clean clothes, and I like the smell of freshly washed clothes.

Day 70

I am very thankful to feel loved on Valentine's Day.

Well, we share cards in school, and I feel loved! It is a great feeling, and I want everybody in this world to feel loved.

Day 71

I am so thankful to have Google. It has answers to almost everything.

What are you grateful for today?

Day 72

I am thankful that God created Moms!

Day 73

I am very thankful to have a long day at the beach.

It is so much fun at the beach. I wish we had a beach in our school.

Day 74

I am so thankful to have showers.

It is a good feeling to take a shower and feel fresh.

Day 75

I am very thankful for street food.

I love to stand by a cart and eat street food.

Day 76

I am thankful for hot dogs.

My favorite kind are Polish sausages!

Day 77

I am thankful for the Country Fair at my school. It is such a fun day at the Country Fair. I love to take part in the games, and try to win stuff.

Day 78

I am thankful for homemade greeting cards.

I love to make art projects!

Day 79

I am thankful to be helpful to someone.

I always try to help my friends. It gives me a good feeling.

Day 80

I am thankful to put a smile on my friends' faces. I find such joy if I can help someone and make them happy. I do that to my friends all the time.

Day 81

I am thankful to Dr. Seuss for his books.

It is fun to read his books.

Day 82

I am thankful to have a long weekend.

I do not have to go to school for three days. It is nice to take a break from school sometimes.

Day 83

I am thankful for camera phones. You get to take photos anywhere.

Day 84

I am so thankful for staying healthy when most of my friends in my class have a cold.

It is not a good feeling once you get a cold.

Day 85

I am thankful for all the bake shops.

Well, Mom and I go to these places to have treats.

Day 86

I am thankful to go on a cruise.

It was my first time on a cruise.

It was so much fun to be in the ocean.

Day 87

I am thankful to build a birdhouse.

Dad and I did this craft on the weekend. I did most of the work, and it was fun to see how everything came together.

What are you thankful for?

Day 88

Nature is all around us! Explore the beauty of nature and write down what you are grateful for.

I get to
see
birds
different
colours
that
makes
me
happy
and
thankful.

Day 89

I am thankful to have my dog Butterball, and for all the love he gives me! Whenever he sees me, he comes running, and gives me lots of kisses to show his love.

Day 90

I am thankful for summer breaks.

There is no school in summertime, and I go to different summer camps, and I like that.

Day 91

I am very thankful today. I went with Mom to a grocery store.

The clerk was very nice, and gave us service with a smile.

Day 92

I am thankful for my family photos. It is so much fun to look at the old baby photos with my family.

Share below your favourite family memory.

Day 93

I am thankful for art books.

I love to do art, so it is fun to do some interesting art in these books.

Day 94

I am so thankful for good memories.

Day 95

I love hugs from my Nana.

My Nana is always content. I never see her upset. I love it when she hugs me.

Day 96

I am thankful for sand, sea and sunsets. I love to play in the sand, swim in the sea, and love watching sunsets.

Day 97

I am thankful for writing paper. We use lots of paper for so many things, like to draw and write on.

Day 98

I am thankful to my homeroom teacher. She is so much fun and makes us all have fun and learn at the same time.

Day 99

I am thankful to have a window seat in a restaurant. It is a better seat, and gives me a chance to look out.

Day 100

I am thankful for the baby tooth under my pillow. The tooth fairy comes and leaves me a present!

Day 101

I am thankful for all the toys I received this year.

I love to play with toys. They take me to a different world.

Day 102

I am so thankful that we are going to Mexico this year.

It will be fun to see a different country.

Day 103

I am thankful for Easter dinners. We get together with family and friends, and have a big feast.

Day 104

I am very thankful to sleep on a nice pillow at night.

It is a very comfortable feeling, and I am lucky to have a pillow because people sleeping on the streets must not be comfortable.

Day 105

I am thankful to my love of dance.

I love to dance, and want to learn many types of dances.

Day 106

I am thankful for heated swimming pools.

It is not fun to swim in a cold pool.

Day 107

I am so thankful to all the unconditional love from my dog.

No matter what I do with him, he still wags his tail for me, and he is so much fun. I treat him like another family member, because he is one.

Day 108

I am thankful for the pancakes that my Mom makes.

She makes the best chocolate pancakes!

I'm most grateful for the car accident that left me paralyzed when I was 15 years old. The accident forever changed me physically, but it also altered the course of my life, making me stronger mentally and emotionally.

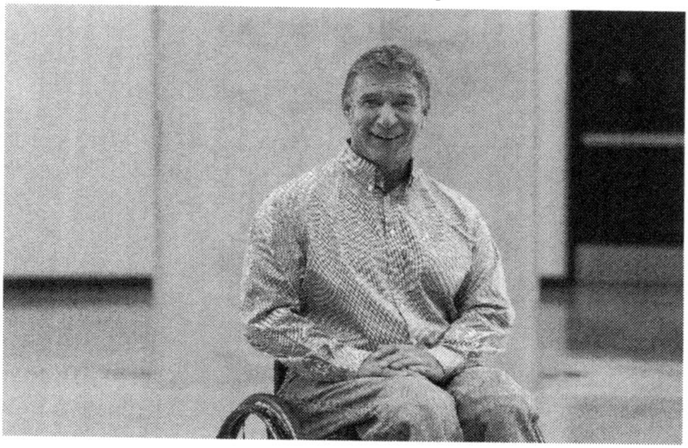

Photo by: Hayley Dryhurst

The accident started me on my journey to remove barriers for people with disabilities and allowed me to make a difference in this world. I am truly grateful to be on this continuing journey, and of course, for my wonderful family, my wife and three incredible daughters.

~ *Rick Hansen, Rick Hansen Foundation* ~

Rick Hansen is CEO of the Rick Hansen Foundation and a passionate advocate for people with disabilities in Canada and around the world. After becoming paralyzed at the age of 15, Rick went on to become a celebrated Paralympic athlete, winning 19 international wheelchair marathons, as well as two gold, two silver and one bronze medal at the 1984 and 1980 summer games.

Following his athletic career, Rick embarked on the *Man In Motion World Tour*, an epic two-year wheelchair trip around the world to prove the potential of people with disabilities and raise awareness for accessibility. This journey was just the beginning of Rick's mission to improve the lives of people with disabilities and prove that anything is possible if you have the courage to try.

Since the *Man In Motion World Tour*, Rick has dedicated his life to creating a world that is accessible and inclusive for all by removing barriers for people with disabilities. Rick and his team at the Foundation are working hard to change attitudes, create accessible spaces and liberate the amazing potential of people with disabilities.

www.rickhansen.com

Day 109

I am simply thankful for happy times.

It is so nice to have happy times and love everyone.

Day 110

I am so thankful for finding song lyrics on the Internet.

I love to sing, so whenever I want to learn a new song I simply go on the Internet and print out the lyrics.

Day 111

I am thankful for my sweet dreams.

They keep me happy all day.

What did you dream about last night?

Write or draw below!

Day 112

I am so thankful to make friends and exchange ideas with them.

When in class, we work together; and we share so many ideas that are fun.

Day 113

I am thankful to special people.

You learn so much from them. Mom reads me biographies of so many great leaders or good people.

Day 114

I am so thankful for a fresh and tangy lemon. I love to eat lemons, just like that. It is fun.

Day 115

I am thankful to have hot chocolate with big marshmallows in it.

Whenever it is cold outside, I like to warm myself up with this special treat!

Day 116

I am just thankful for little things. It is a good feeling to be thankful!

What are you thankful for today? How about yesterday? Write it on this page!

Day 117

I am thankful I got to go and buy flowers. I went with Dad to buy flowers, and it is fun to look at different kinds.

Write down the most important gratitude you have.

Day 118

I have so much fun jumping, and have lots of playtime with my friends. How lucky I am! Which friends are you grateful for? Write their names down and tell them how grateful you are for their presence in your life!

Day 119

I am so thankful to see a beautiful rainbow in the sky.

It makes me wonder how many colors there are, and how pretty it looks.

Day 120

I am thankful for the feeling of being blessed.

I am always paying attention to what I have, so there are tons of things that I am happy and thankful for.

Day 121

I am so thankful to think good thoughts.

It is fun to think good thoughts rather than think thoughts that are not good.

Day 122

I am thankful to my Mom who asked me to write one thing every day that I am thankful for.

I am thinking Mom will be so surprised that I am thankful for many things.

Day 123

I am very thankful for story time.

I love when my parents and sometimes my Nana share stories with me from their childhood.

Day 124

I am so thankful for an unexpected letter.

One day, I got a letter with my name on it that I was not expecting. It sure made me happy!

Day 125

I am thankful for all the bubble baths!

I love taking bubble baths and playing in the tub for so long.

Day 126

I am thankful to smell a bakery from the street.

Sometimes we are walking on the street and you smell fresh baked goods I love that.

Day 127

I am thankful to give thanks for what I have.

I always look around every day, to see what can I find to be thankful for.

Day 128

I am thankful for my eyes.

I can see with my eyes. There is so much to see in the world. When I see people who cannot see, I feel thankful.

Day 129

I am so thankful that I travel to different countries, and am able to learn about foreign cultures.

It gives me a chance to see how life is different everywhere.

Day 130

I am very thankful for all the road trips I get to go on with my family.

I love long car rides, plus we talk and share ideas.

Day 131

I am thankful that I get to take part in different kinds of activities. That makes me a better learner, and also it gives me the chance to meet so many friends.

Day 132

I am so thankful to play in such
beautiful parks in my country.

We are so fortunate to have such
amazing parks, and I love playing there.

Day 133

I am so thankful to play on all the beaches with my family.

I love playing in the water, especially swimming in the ocean, playing with sand and building sand castles is fun.

Day 134

I am thankful to Santa Claus for bringing all the presents and toys for Christmas.

It is so much fun to open presents and getting a picture with Santa.

Day 135

I am thankful for all the

walks with my family.

It is so much fun walking and looking at different areas.

Day 136

I am thankful to put my ideas on paper.

My Mom asked me to write every day, one thing I am thankful for because I was thinking so much how there are so many things that are not right in the world.

Now I am happy to see so much good in the world.

Day 137

I am thankful for all the Autumn feasts.

We get to have so much food and fun with family.

Day 138

I am so thankful to have an education. It will make me a better person.

Day 139

I am thankful for the fresh air.

I love breathing this fresh air we have. I breathed polluted air when we went to India.

Day 140

I am so thankful to my Nana for all the gifts she gives me.

It makes me feel loved.

Day 141

I am thankful for all the treats I get.

Every time I do something good, we celebrate with a treat!

Day 142

I am so thankful for all the holiday cookies we bake.

It is so much fun to bake these cookies and decorate them, but the best part is eating them.

Day 143

I am thankful for the idea that I will have my own charity, as I grow up.

Day 144

I am thankful to play go hide and seek.

It is a fun game.

Day 145

I am so thankful for thick sweaters during winter.

They keep me warm on a cold day.

Day 146

I am thankful to 3D movies.

It is so much fun to watch a 3D movie.

I like to wear those glasses that they give you in the theaters.

Day 147

I am so thankful to victory shouts.

When I play basketball and someone scores, I love that feeling of shouting it out loud.

Day 148

I am thankful to the jumbo chocolate chip cookie. I think about the kids on the streets. They don't even have enough food to eat never mind cookies. So I am thankful and I love chocolate.

I am

thankful

to

Jumbo

chocolate

chip cookie.

Day 149

I am thankful for chocolate milk.

It tastes so good, especially when I pour in extra chocolate syrup.

Day 150

I love to see daisies dancing in the breeze.

There are so many daisies in our garden. When it is windy, it seems like they are dancing. I love watching that.

Day 151

I am so thankful for my cheerfulness.

I love this because nothing bothers me for long, except the fact that there is gender inequality, and also that not all kids can go to school.

Day 152

I am so thankful for my Nana's warm hugs after a long day.

My Nana, is very loving, she is waiting for me at the door when I come from school and hugs me.

It is very refreshing.

Day 153

I am thankful for silent prayers.

I do that every morning.

It feels good to have faith.

Day 154

I am so thankful to buy summer sandals.

It is fun to go out to buy sandals, and try different sandals.

Day 155

I am thankful for cupcakes. I love cupcakes.

It is one of my favourite desserts!

Day 156

I am thankful for teddy bears.

I love to play with them and hug them.

Day 157

I am so thankful for my first time in a foreign country.

I was able to compare the lifestyle difference, and I am lucky to know the difference.

Day 158

I am thankful to be a kid and play.

I am sure adults want to do it too, but cannot play the way a kid can play.

Day 159

I am thankful for my little bedroom library in the house.

I have the choice and collection of books including "I am Malala."

Day 160

I am so thankful for late Sunday breakfasts. It is fun to get up late and eat breakfast late.

Day 161

I am so thankful for alarm clocks.

It helps us to wake up in the morning at a certain time.

Day 162

I am so thankful to sing to the different songs on the radio when we drive.

I love singing. It is so much fun to sing in the car.

Day 163

I am thankful for my pretty face.

I love my pretty face and thank God for making me the way I am.

Draw your pretty face below!

Day 164

I am so thankful to all the firefighters we have.

These are the people who put their lives in danger to save others.

Day 165

I am thankful for watching seedlings grow on the windowsill of our kitchen.

It is fun to watch that. I planted a bean seed, and I waited for few days, watered every day. It was nice to do all that.

Day 166

I am thankful for the glass of water at bedtime.

It is so nice to have water by your bedside. I think of the families in some countries who have to go far away to get water.

Day 167

I am so thankful to get farm fresh food.

I love to go to the farm market with my Mom and Dad!

Day 168

I am so thankful to making dreams in bed. You go to sleep, and seems like you go to some other land through your dreams.

Day 169

I am thankful for the warmth when you need it.

In cold winters, it is good to get warm in cozy clothes.

Day 170

I am thankful for rainfalls.

If it doesn't rain, how will we water every tree and plant?

Day 171

I am thankful to GPS in cars.

It takes you anywhere you need to go.

Day 172

I am thankful for Halloween.

You get to dress up in your favourite costumes and get so many candies.

Day 173

Our house had a break-in.

They took lots of things.

I am thankful that all of us are safe and here.

Day 174

I am so thankful for my helpfulness.

I am always ready to help without being asked because I love helping others.

Day 175

I am thankful for all my friends.

We play and sometimes don't get along,

but it is nice to have good friends.

Day 176

I am thankful for all the fruit trees in my backyard.

Why? It is good to eat organic fruits.

What did you find today that you are grateful for?

Day 177

I am thankful to the garbage collectors.

They help keep our house garbage free.

Day 178

I am thankful to have lots of stuffed animals. On a really hot day, my Mom gave a ride to a lady who had three small kids. She was asking for some toys, so I gave them lots of my stuffed toys, and that makes me feel blessed.

I am
thankful
to
have
lots of
stuffed
animals.

Day 179

I am thankful for electricity.

We have a lot of things that run on power, so I am thankful to have it.

Day 180

I am thankful that I can walk.

I see kids in wheelchairs.

Day 181

I am thankful to have a heart that is always wanting to help.

Day 182

I am thankful that I am not a picky eater. I hear adults saying they are picky eaters.

Day 183

I am thankful to have a good night's sleep.

It freshens me up for another day.

Day 184

I am thankful to have a good breakfast in the morning.

I heard over the radio that some kids don't get to have breakfast in the morning.

Day 185

I am thankful to know how to play tennis.

My Dad plays good tennis, and I love playing with him.

Day 186

I am thankful for good music.

Music is my favorite thing.

Day 187

I am thankful that I don't complain about getting up early.

It is easy for Mom to wake me up. Actually, I am excited to have another fun filled day.

Day 188

I am thankful for sour candies.

My Mom and I love sour candies.

Day 189

I am thankful that my Nana makes the best yogurt.

I love eating yogurt and the one she makes is the best!

Day 190

I am thankful to be able to listen to my parents' childhood memories. It makes me happy to know how life was different back then.

Day 191

I am thankful for every new day.

It is a fresh start, and it gives you a chance to live another day in your life.

Day 192

I am thankful to be an only child.

It is a good feeling even though sometimes I think it would be nice to have a sibling.

Day 193

I am thankful for all the silly things I do.

It is fun to be a kid.

Day 194

I am thankful to learn new

things every day.

There is so much to do. I like it.

Day 195

I am thankful for all the songs that birds sing every morning.

It is so amazing to hear them very early in the morning. It is like a song to me, not sure if they are talking or singing.

Day 196

I am thankful for the casual days at school.

There's no need to wear our uniform, and we normally collect money and other things for good causes.

I am most the grateful for the feeling, the knowing, the remembering that we are not separate. We are the same. And not just in the "we all bleed red" type of way. A deeper same. We are like your two hands that seem separate, but are part of the same body. I am most grateful that we are one... and that I get to spend my time sharing that good news.

Photo by: Chris Dowsett

~ Taylor Conroy, Change Heroes ~

Taylor is a disruptive social entrepreneur whose social enterprise 'Change Heroes' (changeheroes.com) has funded over 250 projects to date, including schools, libraries, girls scholarships, anti-sex trafficking work, and clean water systems, which will impact over 150,000 people in 13 developing countries around the world. Change Heroes won 'Best Social Enterprise' at the StartUp World Finals in San Francisco. By partnering with some of the world's largest nonprofits including Free The Children, Partners in Health, CARE USA and the United Nations Foundation, as well as companies like Morgan Stanley, Disney, and Royal Bank of Canada, Change Heroes is effecting scalable change where it is needed most.

As a speaker, Taylor has presented around the world to over 100,000 people. He has regularly been invited to present at the United Nations and has lectured on social entrepreneurship at Harvard, Princeton, NYU, Cornell, and Stanford. He has studied meditation with Zen monks in Japan, surfed the longest wave in the world in Peru, filmed documentaries in Cambodia, Uganda, and Ecuador, become a yoga teacher in Costa Rica, run with the bulls in Spain, travelled to 35 countries, and explored every continent on earth.

Day 197

I am very thankful for the morning assemblies at school.

It is nice to get together as a school like a family, and learn new things by listening to teachers and watching some video clips.

Day 198

I am thankful to see old people walking on the streets.

It is nice that they get out and get fresh air.

Day 199

I am thankful to see Autumn colours and leaves falling.

This tells me Autumn is here, and I love to see the leaves change colours.

Day 200

I am thankful for my substitute teachers.

They are there when our teachers cannot be.

Day 201

I am thankful to stay up late nights.

It is fun and there's no rush to go to bed early.

Day 202

I am so thankful that I can move my fingers.

Some people do not have fingers and some cannot move them.

Trace your hand below!

Day 203

I am thankful that I could finally draw a snowflake with six sides. I have been trying that for a long time, and was only making it with four sides.

Day 204

I am so thankful to the people who smile at you when you make eye contact with them.

It is a good feeling to see happy people.

Day 205

I am thankful to hear the TV noise.

That means Dad is home.

Day 206

I am thankful to watch my Mom making breakfast early mornings.

It is a good feeling to see her making a good breakfast for the family.

What are you thankful for today?

Day 207

I am thankful for my beautiful long hair, so I could donate it to a Cancer Agency to make wigs. I believe in sharing, and I know when people get diagnosed with cancer they lose hair. I am thankful that someone will get a wig made with my hair, and that makes me feel happy.

I am
thankful to
my
beautiful
long
hair
so I
could
donate
it to
the
cancer
agency.

Day 208

I am thankful to see happy and kind people.

They are happy, and make others happy.

Day 209

I am thankful to treat everyone I meet with courtesy and respect.

This is the way I am.

Day 210

I am thankful to invent a new dance.

Sometimes I can come up with a crazy dance.

Day 211

I am so thankful to have ice cream for dessert.

Who wouldn't be?

Day 212

I am thankful to take part in school concerts.

It is fun to be a team player.

Day 213

I am thankful to have Silly Putty.

It is so much fun to play with it.

Day 214

I am so thankful for family values.

I hear stories about my grandparents and am happy that my parents have the same values and now I am learning those.

Write down below what you are thankful for.

Day 215

I am happy to have hands, so I can do so many things including writing my thoughts.

Day 216

I am thankful to watch a movie.

You learn so much from movies, and have fun at the same time.

Day 217

I am thankful for Sunday brunch buffets

You get up late and go out

and have a good buffet.

It is one of my favorite things to do.

Day 218

I am thankful to admit when I am wrong.

That means I am learning from my mistakes.

Day 219

I am thankful for a special

weekend event.

It is fun.

Write down a fun memory you have

below!

Day 220

I am very thankful for the watering can.

I water my plants and flowers with it.

Day 221

I am thankful for the pilots

They take us around the world.

Day 222

I am thankful for the pullout trays in the planes.

I am just thankful to have everything.

Day 223

I am thankful to Santa Claus and all the holidays, just because he makes so many people happy and holidays bring people together.

Day 224

I am thankful that my grandparents came to Canada.

It is a beautiful place to live in.

Day 225

I am thankful to learn astronomy.

I am starting to learn about this, and it is just amazing.

Day 226

I am thankful for beach front vacations.

You hear the sea at night and get up and play all day on the beach.

Day 227

I am so thankful for comfy chairs

in big book stores.

It is nice to sit and read there.

Day 228

I am so thankful for apple blossoms.

They are lovely to see.

Day 229

I am thankful for high chairs for babies.

I used to sit in one and eat comfortably. My Mom told me stories, and I saw in my baby pictures, too.

Day 230

I am very thankful to have a bubble bath today. I like to play with my duckies for a long time.

Day 231

I am so thankful to my family who
treats my friends with love.

Whenever my best friend comes over,
I always feel that she gets treated the
same as me.

Day 232

I am thankful to the Easter bunny.

I like him because he leaves so many eggs for me.

Day 233

I am so thankful for learning how to write cursive.

It is exciting to learn new things.

Day 234

I am thankful for Oreo cookies.

That is my favorite cookie.

Day 235

I am thankful to work things out on my own. I am in Grade 3, so I like to do things on my own.

Day 236

I am so thankful to have a computer.

It is a good thing to have if you use it wisely, which I do.

Who are you most grateful for in your life?

Day 237

I am so thankful that I am a girl.

I hear our family and friends who only have boys, talking about and wishing they had one girl, so I am happy to be a girl.

our family
friends who
only have
boys often
says "we
wish we
had one
girl" so
girls must
be special.

Day 238

I am thankful for magic shows.

It is interesting to see how they do magic.

Day 239

I am thankful for hula hooping.

I can finally do it.

Day 240

I am thankful to go back to

school after holidays.

It is good to have fun, but school is

important, and I love my school.

Day 241

I am thankful for having clothes.

I like to dress up, but some people in other countries don't even have clothes.

Day 242

I am so thankful for quiet libraries.

Some libraries can be noisy, so it's nice to find one with a quiet place to read.

Day 243

I am so thankful to make a horse gallop.

I love to ride a horse, and yesterday I could make my horse gallop.

It is so exciting!

Day 244

I am so thankful to my Mom for getting me a journal. Now, I am able to write my thoughts of gratitude.

Day 245

I am thankful for board games.

Sometimes, we take board games to school. It is fun, and I like to play with my family too.

Day 246

I am thankful for Caesar salad.

That is one of my favourite salads.

Day 247

I am thankful to make my own waffles.

I love waffles, and when I make mine, I put lots of syrup and whipping cream on them.

Day 248

I am thankful to have such a nice airport.

I have seen many airports, but Vancouver airport is the best.

Day 249

I am so thankful for art in everyday life. If you look closely, there is art everywhere.

Day 250

I am thankful for mint chocolate.

It is my favourite.

Day 251

I am thankful I'm able to

drink fresh juice.

My Mom makes the best fresh

juice in the morning.

Day 252

I am thankful for all my dolls.

I love playing with dolls,

it is my favorite thing.

Day 253

I am thankful for turkey dinners.

I love eating turkey, and getting together with friends and family to celebrate.

One of the best parts is having turkey soup the next day.

Day 254

I am thankful for all the breakfast smoothies.

They taste good, and you can drink them on the way to school, too.

Day 255

I am thankful for all the prizes I won.

We went to the Pacific National Exhibition and had a great time.

Day 256

I am thankful for being strong and getting over life's challenges like a test.

Day 257

I am thankful for a beautiful ferry ride.

We went to Victoria and had so much fun exploring!

Day 258

I am thankful to learn in a group.

It is good to share ideas. I enjoy working in groups in my school.

Day 259

I am so thankful for walking tours.

When we travel, sometimes we walk with the guide in a group.

Day 260

I am thankful for the blanket that keeps me warm.

Well, it is fun to watch TV on cold winter nights under your favorite blanket.

Day 261

I am thankful to look for good things all the time.

Mom told me to look for what is good in the world because I was upset that not all girls can go to school, and also why girls cannot be accepted in families like boys.

Day 262

I am thankful that I can find things that are good. I can't wait to see what Mom's reaction will be once I tell her that I have been writing my thoughts.

Day 263

I am thankful to know how to skate. We went skating today, and it was fun.

Day 264

I am thankful to be a good girl.

I am a girl who wants to make a difference!

Day 265

I am thankful to know how to convince my Dad to buy me a treat.

He will sometimes first say "No"; but then, he later agrees.

Day 266

I am so thankful to have dinner on the shore. We had dinner at a restaurant that serves food on the shore.

What are you most grateful for today?

Day 267

I am so thankful that I am absolutely unique. I am so happy all the time, and always ready to help. I think that makes me unique.

I am
so thankful
to
be
absolutely
unique.

Day 268

I am thankful for pizza nights.

I love eating pizza on lazy nights with my family.

Day 269

I am thankful to eat organic eggs.

They taste so good.

Day 270

I am thankful for the first day back at school.

It is good to go to a new grade.

Day 271

I am so thankful for honey sticks.

We buy honey from a farm that sells honey sticks.

Day 272

I am so thankful for bird nests.

Aren't birds creative how they can make their little homes?

Day 273

I am thankful for sunglasses.

They protect my eyes from the sun.

Day 274

I am thankful for my helpfulness.

I am always ready to help.

Day 275

I am thankful for pajama day at school. You don't feel like you are going to school because you are not wearing your uniform.

Day 276

I am thankful to be acknowledged for my hard work. I really work hard, and when I achieve my goal it fills my heart with joy!

Day 277

I am thankful for summer camps.

I love going to summer camps and my favorite is horseback riding

Day 278

I am so thankful for thank you notes.

It is so nice to say thank you with a simple note.

Day 279

I am thankful to watch so many crows flying together.

When I go to school sometimes there are so many crows flying together and I wonder what they are doing.

Day 280

I am thankful for sofa beds.

It is two in one.

Day 281

I am very thankful for cotton candy.

It is fun to eat and I like different colors,

but my favorite is pink!

Day 282

I am thankful when Mom

gets mad at me.

That way, I learn not to make the same

mistake again.

Day 283

I am thankful for the great chicken

Mom makes.

My Mom makes really good food, and

makes the best chicken.

Day 284

I am thankful that I got a

new handbag today.

My parents know I love handbags, and I did well in school, so I got another handbag.

Day 285

I am thankful to people who

give good service.

When you go to a hotel there are people

who make you feel at home.

Day 286

I am thankful when your friend is listening to you.

When you share a story with a friend, and she listens without interrupting.

Day 287

I am thankful to be able to play dress up with my best friend.

My best friend came over and it was so much fun!

Day 288

I am thankful for who I am!!

Are you thankful for you? Write why on this page!

Day 289

I am thankful for all the trees in my backyard.

Day 290

I am so thankful to decorate our Christmas tree. It is so much fun to decorate it with some beautiful decorations.

Day 291

I am thankful to buy a Mother's Day present for my mom.

It makes me happy.

Day 292

I am thankful for piggy banks.

I have so many different shapes of piggy banks.

Day 293

I am thankful for the kids who behave.

Sometimes, I see kids not really listening to their parents.

Day 294

I am thankful for the last day of school.

It is nice to take a break before
Christmas or summer.

Day 295

I am thankful for all I do.

I make mistakes, and sometimes I do well, so I love it all.

Day 296

I am thankful for all the visits to malls with my parents.

It is fun to spend time together.

Day 297

I am so thankful to open my eyes this morning. It is a good feeling to wake up in the morning and think how you will spend your day.

I know
I am
so beautiful
not the
way I
look but
the way
I think.

Day 298

I am thankful I have an American Doll.

She looks like me, and sometimes we wear the same clothes.

Day 299

I am thankful to earn a medal

in Chess today.

Chess is a fun game, and I am proud of

my hard work.

Day 300

I am thankful to earn a merit today at school.

I felt good, and will try to do even better in school.

Day 301

I am thankful for riding around on my bike with my Dad.

It gives me a chance to be with Daddy, and we love bike rides.

Day 302

I am thankful for movie nights with my friends!

We always have lots of fun.

Day 303

I am thankful for all the happy times.

It is good to have happy times.

Day 304

I am thankful to my school, principal, teachers, parents and my fellow students who helped me to raise money for the Malala Fund and Rick Hansen Foundation.

It would not have been possible to do it if they all didn't help me. It would have been just an idea. But with their help it is a reality now.

Day 305

I am thankful to have such heart to help others.

When I grow up, I want to help so much and so many people.

Day 306

I am thankful to the box that I made to collect money from our family and friends at home. I wrote down on that box the name of my charity, "Helping Hands" and even made a logo. I will have my charity to help everyone I can.

Day 307

I am thankful to get all the support I have from everyone.

I said before it would have been just an idea if my family and friends did not support me.

Day 308

I am thankful for all the love that I have in my heart for everyone.

I love everyone without wanting anything in return, so I am lucky.

Day 309

I am so thankful to the waitress who gave us such good service.

We went to a restaurant today and it was an amazing experience because of the food, and the waitress made it even better.

Day 310

I am thankful to the unkind people.

Why? Well, they are showing their emotion.

My Mom says showing emotions is a good thing, but we should still be kind.

Day 311

I am thankful for flip-flops.

It is fun to wear them.

Day 312

I am so thankful for all the kind people in the world.

They make this world a better place.

Day 313

I am thankful for all my Tae Kwon Do Academy awards.

It means I work hard to receive them.

Day 314

I am thankful to all the treats I get

when I do good.

My parents reward me.

Day 315

I am thankful for craft shops.

I love doing crafts.

Day 316

I am thankful for all the pineapple we had in Maui.

It was very tasty, and was better than the ones we buy from the supermarket.

Day 317

I am thankful for positive people, and those who are caring.

They are fun people to be around with, and they also love animals.

Day 318

I am thankful to the seniors who come to visit us at our school.

They come for Christmas concerts, and I like to see them happy.

Day 319

I am so thankful to have food on the table every day.

I know so many people go to sleep hungry. I see kids digging into garbage, so how can I take things for granted?

Day 320

I am thankful to drink hot chocolate.

In cold weather, it tastes good and

warms you up too.

Day 321

I am thankful to sing happy songs, especially in the bathroom. I am just so thankful for everything now since I learnt that some girls are not welcomed in the family.

Day 322

I am thankful for the hot lunch we have at school on Wednesdays.

It is good to have hot lunch.

Day 323

I am thankful for the alarm system.

I feel safe when the alarm is on.

Day 324

I am thankful to play all day today.

I had no school today.

Day 325

I am thankful for my funny self.

I am always happy and make everyone around me happy.

Day 326

I am thankful to bring-a-friend days at my ballet dance.

It is fun to dance with a friend.

What are you thankful for?

Day 327

I am thankful to work toward my goal.

It is very rewarding to get to my goal to get better at something, or to share something like my hair, which I donated to kids who have cancer.

I belive
in sharing
and
I know
when
people get
diagnosed
with cancer
they
lose hair
and I am
happy
I could
help.

Day 328

I am thankful to have a friend coming over.

It is so much fun to be with a friend, and do silly things.

Day 329

I am thankful to my silly self.

I'm silly and play around a lot and Mom says, "Go get your sillys out!"

Day 330

I am thankful for art classes.

I love art, and it gives me a good feeling once I make something good.

Day 331

I am thankful to my Mom who teaches me good lessons.

Every morning, when we go to school, there is this old lady walking very slowly on the road. Mom stops the car and makes me wish the lady "Good morning!" I like being kind to everyone!

Day 332

I am thankful for learning from everyone. I think it will make me a better adult.

Day 333

I am thankful to see all the good things around me.

I now pay attention to it all the time because it's nice to appreciate all of the blessings.

Day 334

I am very thankful to have such good parents.

It is very important.

Day 335

I am thankful to go to bed before I get too sleepy.

I like to read in bed, so if I am too sleepy, I won't be able to read.

Day 336

I am thankful to write a song.

I was able to write some beautiful words, so I am very thankful.

Day 337

I am very thankful to big beach balls.

They are tons of fun to play with.

Day 338

I am so very thankful to reflect back on life, and find what is good.

I was only looking at what is not good in the world, but by looking for good surprised me because I have more things that I am thankful for.

Day 339

I am very thankful for all the bike rides with my family.

Spending time with family is fun.

Day 340

I am always thankful to say

something nice.

I love this about myself.

Day 341

I am thankful for all the daily reminders.

It helps me to keep track of my day.

Day 342

I am thankful to my dog's squeaky toys.

It is like music to my ears, when he plays with those toys because it makes him so happy!

Day 343

I am thankful for the rocking chair in my bedroom.

Day 344

I am very thankful to have so many piggy banks.

I love putting change in them.

Day 345

I am thankful for talking to the animals in the Zoo.

I feel they can understand me.

Day 346

I am thankful to watch it snow.

In some hot countries, kids never get to see snow.

Day 347

I am thankful to stack books in the order I want to read them.

Mom reads so many books to me. I love to plan which one we should read next.

Day 348

I am thankful for the feeling I get when my best friend visits me.

She moved away from me, so it is nice to have her back every now and then.

Day 349

I am thankful for bathing suit season. It is fun to play in the water and get wet.

Day 350

I am thankful to pay close attention to everything.

I love to be curious.

Day 351

I am thankful to take a hike

It is fun to go for hikes.

You get to see new places.

Day 352

I am thankful that my Mom can read my mind.

Sometimes I don't even have to speak, and she knows what I want to say.

Day 353

I am thankful for watermelons.

I love eating watermelon!

Day 354

I am thankful for getting off a plane after a long flight.

It is very tiring to go for long plane rides.

Day 355

I am thankful to have an American Doll store in Seattle now. I love to go there for my doll. It is a fun place to be.

Day 356

I am thankful for doll strollers. I like to take my doll in a stroller to the mall and on long walks.

What were you thankful for yesterday?

Day 357

I am thankful to be born as a girl.

I think girls are amazing; nothing against boys but we are awesome!

I am

thankful

to

be

a

girl.

Day 358

I am very thankful for room service.

I love to have food in a room after a long travel.

Day 359

I am thankful for making up songs.

It is fun! Mom and I sometimes make up our own song while driving to school.

Day 360

I am so thankful for the late starts in school after holidays.

School will start late after holidays, and it is easy, so we don't have to get up early.

Day 361

I am thankful to the gift of every day.

It is a blessing to be here on this planet
and I always look forward to a new day.

Day 362

I am so thankful to meet new teachers every year. I am learning a lot from them and they take good care of me while I am away from my family.

Day 363

I am so thankful to receive so much love from everyone in my family.

It is such a good feeling to be loved.

I wish for everyone to feel loved.

Day 364

I am so thankful to be witty and confident. I am never afraid to take on new challenges.

Day 365

I am so thankful to the Universe and this beautiful planet earth we live in.

I am so amazed to know how big it is.

Afterword

There's a story I heard once about a large truck that got stuck beneath an overpass, causing a traffic jam. A host of experts were called out to review the situation and to find a solution that would free the truck. For hours, the smartest men and women were dispatched to see what they could do and still the truck sat there, stuck under the bridge. A young child who had been sitting in the traffic jam got out of her car and walked up to see the truck. She tried in vain to get the attention of the adults until finally she tugged on the jacket of a police officer. "What is it?" the officer asked, irritated at the interruption from his busy thoughts. "The tires," the young child replied. "Let the air out of the tires."

That's the funny thing about spirituality: we tend to complicate it. With voluminous texts, wordy dissertations, and intricate modalities, we often take the simple art of living joyfully and turn it into a complex science. In the process, we miss the obvious. We overlook the simple solutions, and like the truck and the overpass find ourselves stuck within the stress of trying to do spirituality correctly, while blind to the simple solutions.

This book is a treasure… a simple book written from an innocent heart, wonderfully naïve to the complexities of the subject matter, and thus offering us an opportunity to find the joy hiding in plain sight in our everyday lives. With 365 simple reminders to embrace life, to breathe, to laugh, and to be grateful for the moments we have, we are reminded to let the air out of our stressful lives and, for a moment, savor the simple things all around us.

Muskan shines a light on the pure and beautiful truth for which we all long. Unlike self-help books and how-to manuals, she doesn't do so by showing us the way; instead, because she is a child, she simply holds a space and writes from the purity of childhood. This book isn't good because it was written by a young person. It's not a novelty or gimmick. Rather, its value comes from the fact that the author hasn't been polluted by the cynicism of adulthood. It's the wisdom of innocence that transports us back to a time and place where we still believed that love and peace were possible. And it's that innocence that ultimately makes this book so powerful.

Reading this book, viewing the world through Muskan's heart, and allowing myself to be impacted by the beauty of youth has reminded me of the essence of my own spirituality and sharing. We all want to be happy, to be safe, to feel loved. That's what 365 Days of Gratitude is all about. In the words of the author: I am so thankful to be a CHILD. Me too.
Big hugs, Jason Garner

Author of … And I Breathed, My Journey from a Life of Matter to a Life That Matters, former CEO of Global Music at Live Nation, and essayist at JasonGarner.com

Photo by: Sara Jordan, Sara Jordan Photography

Jason Garner is a husband, father, former Fortune 500 company executive, and spiritual student who spent the first 37 years of his life working his way up from flea market parking attendant to CEO of Global Music at Live Nation - never taking a breath - in the belief that to be loved he had to be the best. He has worked with rock stars and sports legends and was twice named in Fortune magazine's list of the top 20 highest paid executives under 40.

A series of events centering on the sudden death of his mother from stomach cancer caused him to re-evaluate what really mattered in life ... and to finally breathe. He has spent thousands of hours sitting cross-legged with timeless Masters of mind, body and spirit including learning from the monks at the Shaolin Temple in China. From an open heart and sense of confident vulnerability, he now shares the lessons learned on his journey and what he continues to discover through the daily adventure of life at JasonGarner.com.

About the Author

Muskan came into this world as a miracle after her parents' 16 years of marriage. At the young age of six, Muskan learned about the injustice that Malala Yousafzai had gone through, and was devastated. She was propelled to take action and wanted to make a difference. She started by raising funds to donate to the Malala Fund and other local charities. However, despite the difference she was already making, Muskan didn't want to stop there. She asked her mother incessantly about why there was so much gender inequality in such modern times. In order to shift her thoughts on this subject to a more positive state, her mother gave her a journal and encouraged her to write one thing every day that she was grateful for. She wanted Muskan to focus on all the positive things in her life. As time passed, her mother forgot about the journal, until Muskan came to her later with a journal filled with all of the things she was grateful for and how she had transformed her negative thoughts about gender inequality into positive thoughts on how she can use her influence to make an impact.

From those beautiful daily gratitudes, 365 Days of Gratitude was born. Muskan is inspired by the knowing that her words will make a difference in people's lives and would like to make a difference globally with her charity called *Helping Hands*, whose mission is to help homelessness in every country. Partial proceeds of this very book will be donated to *Helping Hands* as a continued effort in ensuring you are also a part of making a difference.

Muskan lives with her parents and her dog Butterball.

Muskan Virk

When something greater than you send you a message, you sit up and listen! That's what Meera Virk did when one day, she was taking a break from her busy day of being a successful professional in the financial industry. The moment of clarity and knowing that she had experienced at that time was something she said she would never forget and was one of the defining moments of her life. As an already spiritual person with a conscious mindset, Meera had always been aware that there are other possibilities out there. However, she didn't think that her journey would be taking a detour to something that she had only heard about and was at the time not her expertise. She just knew that what was already instilled in her since a little child which was the lesson to help others, was what she is being guided to do.

Inspired throughout the years by Dr. Wayne Dyer, Meera knew that she had to answer the call that would lead to her transformative journey. She immersed herself in her own personal transformation and challenged herself to overcome any barriers that would prevent her in being the best version of her. Her wish for the universe is for future generations to have the conscious connectedness to tap into their own inner wisdom. As a certified Integrative Life Coach Professional ™ she believes that, *"Nothing is permanent, everything is temporary. You have to have that inner wisdom and that is your success. Once you have that, all those other things don't really matter. Don't give up on life and stay connected to your own inner wisdom."*

Meera lives in Vancouver with her husband and daughter, Muskan. As a family, they continue their family mission to be of service and be the voice of others who are homeless.

I'm grateful for…

I'm grateful for…

45192506R00239

Made in the USA
Middletown, DE
27 June 2017